SIMPLY THE BEST
GRILL/GRIDDLE RECIPES

MARIAN GETZ

Copyright © 2015 Marian Getz

Printed in the U.S.A.

ACKNOWLEDGMENTS

A most sincere thank you to our wonderful viewers and customers for without you there would be no need for a cookbook. I try very hard to give you an array of recipes suited for the particular kitchen tool the cookbook is written for. Wolfgang and I create recipes faster than we can write them down. That is what chefs do and is also the reason to tune in to the live shows and even record them so you can learn new dishes that may not be in our cookbooks yet.

Thank you most of all to Wolfgang. You are the most passionate chef I know and it has been a privilege to work for you since 1998. You are a great leader and friend. Your restaurants are full of cooks and staff that have been with you for 20 or more years which is a true testament to how you lead us. Thanks for allowing me to write these cookbooks and for letting me share the stage at HSN with you.

To Greg, my sweet husband since 1983. Working together is a dream and I love you. You have taught me what a treasure it is to have a home filled with laughter.

To my boys, Jordan and Ben, we have a beautiful life, don't we? And it just keeps on getting better since we added Lindsay, J.J. as well as precious Easton and Sadie, our first grand babies.

To all the great people at WP Productions, Syd, Arnie, Mike, Phoebe, Michael, Nicolle, Tracy, Genevieve, Gina, Nancy, Sylvain and the rest of the team, you are all amazing to work with. Watching all the wonderful items we sell develop from idea to final product on live television is an awe-inspiring process to see and I love that I get to be a part of it.

To Daniel Koren, our patient editor and photographer, thank you for your dedication. You make the photo shoot days fun and you are such an easygoing person to work with in the cramped, hot studio we have to share. We have learned so much together and have far more to learn.

To Greg, Cat, Estela, Angi, Laurie, Keith, Maribel and Margarita who are the most dedicated, loving staff anyone could wish for. You are the true heroes behind the scenes. You are a well-oiled machine of very hard working people who pull off the live shows at HSN. It is a magical production to watch, from the first box unpacked, to the thousands of eggs cracked and beaten to running to get that "thing" Wolf asks for at the last minute, to the very last dish washed and put away it is quite a sight to behold. I love you all and I deeply love what we do.

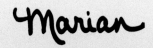

2

Whether you work in a busy restaurant kitchen or prepare family dinners at home, having the right appliances is essential to success in the kitchen. Over the years, I have really come to appreciate the versatility and reliability of the grill and griddle and it has become one of my go-to appliances. In addition to being able to handle hours of continued use, its portability is a wonderful benefit as well.

A student of cooking is probably one of the best ways to describe Marian. She is always looking for something new, something fresh, something local and something seasonal. Her culinary knowledge combined with her passion for cooking is second to none.

Marian's Grill/Griddle Cookbook is a wonderful collection of recipes that I know you will enjoy. She has taken her experiences as a chef, mother, and now grandmother, and created an amazing guide for anyone to be successful in the kitchen. Her recipes are easy to follow, taste incredible and will motivate you to become more creative in the kitchen.

I know that her philosophy of cooking is the same as mine – use great ingredients and make awesome food!

Wolfgang Puck

GRILL RECIPES

TABLE OF CONTENTS

4

GRIDDLE RECIPES

TABLE OF CONTENTS

GRILL/GRIDDLE TIPS

About Your Grill/Griddle

Your grill/griddle is incredibly versatile and it is my hope that you will use it often enough to leave it out on your countertop or your patio. Your grill/griddle can make a vast array of foods in a hurry because the surface is large and heats up so well. You will be able to make breakfast, lunch, dinner, desserts and even snacks on your grill/griddle.

Preheating

The heat up time for the grill/griddle is 10 minutes so I make good use of that time to finish prepping the items I will be cooking. Because the grill/griddle cooks fast, I recommend having all your ingredients within arm's reach before you start cooking.

Cleaning

The clean up of your grill/griddle is very easy due to its wonderful nonstick coating. While it is still slightly warm, place one end of the grill/griddle plate in the sink and use a soft, soapy brush to clean it. If you have a dishwasher large enough to accommodate the grill/griddle plate, you can clean it in there as well. Please refer to the use and care manual that came with your grill/griddle for more details on how to clean and care for it.

Temperature Settings

Your grill/griddle can produce very high heat which makes seasoned cooks very happy for it browns foods so well. If you are new to cooking, I suggest to turn the temperature down a bit until you are used to how fast it cooks. The temperature settings are similar to those on a regular stove. If you don't see a particular temperature setting marked on the adjustable temperature probe of your grill/griddle, go to the closest temperature setting and place the dial halfway between the numbers aiming for the one you want.

Excess Grease Spatter and Smoke

It is advantageous to apply oil to the food rather than the grill/griddle's surface when cooking at high temperatures as this will also help keeping grease spatter and smoke to a minimum.

Please use this chart as a reference for cooking the most common types of food on your grill/griddle. Temperatures may vary depending on the specific recipe or your personal taste. Testing for doneness by temperature is done using a meat thermometer.

Meat	Time/Temperature	Doneness Test
Beefsteaks 1" thick 3/4" thick	10-15 min 450°F	medium-rare - 145°F medium - 160°F well done - 170°F
Burgers 3/4" thick	14-16 min 400°F	medium - 160°F or until no longer pink in the center
Turkey Burgers	15-20 min 400°F	
Pork Chops Rib and Loin 1/2" thick	10-12 min 12-15 min 350°F	160°F or until slightly pink in the center
Pork Ribs Spare Ribs	25-30 min 350°F	160°F or until no longer pink in the center
Sausage Links Hotdogs (cooked)	4-6 min 400°F	140°F or until hot
Bratwurst or other raw sausages	12-15 min 300°F	180°F or until no longer pink in the center
Chicken Bone-In	25-35 min 350°F	until juice in the center is no longer pink
Boneless, skinless breast half	15-20 min 350°F	until juice in the center is no longer pink
Shrimp large, raw, shelled, deveined	8-12 min 350°F	until pink and firm
Fish Whole, drawn & scaled	10 min per 1/2" thick 350°F	160°F or until fish flakes easily with fork
Steaks, 3/4" thick	15-20 min 350°F	160°F or until fish flakes easily with fork
Fillets	10 min per 1/2" thick 350°F	160°F or until fish flakes easily with fork

COOKING TIPS

Raw Meat

When cooking raw meat, be mindful of what you do with your tongs. If you use the same pair of tongs to place raw chicken on the grill then later use them to transfer the cooked chicken to a platter, there is a chance that those tongs may still have live bacteria on them. Either wash them before removing cooked food or use a second pair.

Keeping the Kitchen Clean

When you sear foods on the grill/griddle, they spatter up a fine mist of oil that can get all over your countertop. I suggest lining your countertop with two wide strips of plastic wrap then set the grill/griddle on it. When finished cooking, remove the cooled grill/griddle and peel away the plastic wrap to unveil a spotless countertop.

Searing Meats

In order to ensure proper browning of meats when searing or sautéing, you need to dry it off first. If wet, the heat must first boil away the moisture in the form of steam which starts to boil the food first before it begins to brown it. Wet meat also increases the chance of sticking.

Know your Butcher

If you like to cook but are as busy as I am, I suggest you find a grocery store that still has a real butcher on premise. Make friends with your butcher as a good butcher will save you prep time in the kitchen and make you a better cook because of it. I have my butcher's phone number on speed dial in my phone.

Seasoning Your Food

When grilling savory foods, it is important to season it first. It can be as simple as salt alone or an elaborate array of spices and herbs. Season EVERY BITE of the food by sprinkling the seasonings evenly over the surface of the food. For me, salt and pepper do not always go together. Salt is by far the most important seasoning followed by something tart such as citrus, vinegar, wine, BBQ sauce or mustard that has a tartness to it. It's all about the right balance.

Salt

The salt used in this book is Diamond Crystal Kosher Salt. It is half as salty as most other brands. This is because the grains are very fluffy and therefore not as many fit into a measuring spoon. This brand also lists only "salt" as the ingredient on the box. If you are using salt other than Diamond Crystal Kosher Salt, simply use half the amount specified in the recipe.

Oil and Butter

Use your favorite oil on the grill/griddle. Canola is my favorite neutral-tasting oil and I also like to use olive oil. Try to avoid using extra-virgin olive oil as it has a lower smoke point. High temperatures will ruin its unique fruity flavor. Peanut oil is also a great oil to use if you are not allergic to it. If a recipe calls for butter, I always use the unsalted kind. Salted butter has a longer shelf life as the salt acts as a preservative but it comes at the expense of a taste that is stale compared to that of unsalted butter. Softened butter means butter that has been left at room temperature for several hours. It should be soft enough to offer no resistance whatsoever when sliced using a knife. While there is no perfect substitute for the pure flavor of butter, you can use a substitute such as margarine and most of the recipes will turn out fairly well.

Vanilla

I adore vanilla and order both my vanilla extract and vanilla beans from a supplier directly from the island of Tahiti. I use both of these in recipes where the vanilla flavor takes center stage. In recipes where vanilla is not the star flavor, I use imitation vanilla because it is less expensive and adds the right amount of taste and aroma without overpowering the other flavors. My favorite is an inexpensive imitation flavoring called Magic Line Butter Vanilla Extract. It adds an incredible sweet smell and taste to baked goods.

Chocolate

Buy good quality chocolate and cocoa whenever possible. It is easy to find excellent chocolate at most grocery stores but it is almost impossible to find good quality cocoa powder. I suggest ordering it online.

Sugar Substitute

If you need to use a sugar substitute, my favorite kind is an all-natural product called Zsweet. I get it at my local health food store. While it does not bake as perfectly as regular sugar, it is the best substitute I know. I also like agave and stevia.

PANTRY TIPS

Being prepared to cook the recipes in this book, or any recipe for that matter, is one of the keys to success in the kitchen. Your pantry must be stocked with the basics. We all know how frustrating it can be when you go to the cupboard and what you need is not there. This list includes some of the ingredients you will find in this book and some that we feel are important to always have on hand.

Perishables:

Onions
Garlic
Tomatoes
Carrots
Celery
Ginger
Bell Peppers
White Potatoes
Sweet Potatoes
Squashes
Citrus
Apples
Bananas
Lettuce
Spinach
Fresh Herbs
Green Onions
Milk
Cream Cheese
Parmesan Cheese
Yogurt
Other Cheeses You Like

Spices:

Kosher Salt
Pepper
Bay Leaves
Sage
Oregano
Thyme
Chili Flakes
Cumin Seeds
Curry Powder
Onion Powder
Garlic Powder
Dry Mustard
Ground Cinnamon
Nutmeg
Cloves
Chili Powder

Dry goods:

Sugars
Sugar Substitute
Vanilla
Extracts/Flavorings
Agave Syrup
Canned Tomatoes
Canned Beans
Canned Vegetables
Dried Chilies
Pasta
Lentils
Stocks
Powdered Bouillon
Olives
Ketchup
Mustard
Pickles
Oils
Vinegar
Honey

It is not necessary to have all the items listed at all times. However, if you are feeling creative, adventurous or just following a recipe, it's great to have a good selection in the kitchen.

ROSEMARY
CHICKEN KABOBS

Makes 4 servings

Ingredients:

For the Herb Mixture:

3 tablespoons canola oil

8 garlic cloves, crushed

2 tablespoons dried oregano

2 teaspoons fresh thyme, finely chopped

1 tablespoon lemon juice

Kosher salt and pepper to taste

For the Chicken:

3 boneless, skinless chicken breasts, cut into 1½-inch cub

8 rosemary sprigs

½ cup feta cheese, crumbled

8 fresh mint leaves, julienned

Method:

1. *Preheat the GRILL SIDE to 350°F for 10 MINUTES.*

2. *In a bowl, combine all herb mixture ingredients; mix well.*

3. *Thread 4-5 chicken cubes on each rosemary sprig.*

4. *Brush each kabob with the herb mixture.*

5. *Place kabobs on the GRILL and cook for 3-4 minutes on each side or until internal temperature reaches 165°F degrees on a meat thermometer.*

6. *Serve chicken garnished with feta cheese and mint leaves.*

TIP
You can also make these kabobs with cubed up pork chops instead of chicken.

BACON WRAPPED
CHICKEN BURGERS

Makes 4 servings

Ingredients:

12 ounces ground chicken

Kosher salt and pepper to taste

12 bacon slices, uncooked

4 soft buns

Lettuce and tomatoes, for serving

Method:

1. *Divide the ground chicken into 4 equal patties.*
2. *Season patties with salt and pepper.*
3. *Lay three strips of bacon in a criss-cross fashion over the top of each patty.*
4. *Neatly tuck the bacon ends under each patty.*
5. *Preheat the GRILL SIDE to 325°F for 10 MINUTES.*
6. *Place the patties on the GRILL and cook for 6-7 minutes on each side or until internal temperature reaches 165°F on a meat thermometer.*
7. *Serve on buns with lettuce and tomatoes.*

TIP

My favorite way to dress this burger is with Thousand Island dressing, lettuce and tomato.

GRILLED CHICKEN & BROCCOLI SALAD

Makes 4 servings

Ingredients:

2 boneless, skinless chicken breasts

1 tablespoon canola oil

Kosher salt and pepper to taste

½ head broccoli, cut into 2-inch florets

¼ cup pine nuts, toasted

1 cup croutons

1 cup bottled Italian dressing

Method:

1. *Preheat GRILL SIDE to 350°F for 10 MINUTES.*
2. *Brush the chicken with oil then season with salt and pepper.*
3. *Place chicken on the GRILL and cook for 7-8 minutes on each side or until internal temperature reaches 165°F on a meat thermometer.*
4. *Remove chicken to a cutting board and let rest for 3 minutes.*
5. *Place broccoli on the GRILL.*
6. *When broccoli is lightly browned, transfer from the GRILL to a large bowl.*
7. *Add pine nuts and croutons to the bowl.*
8. *Cut the chicken into small pieces and place into the bowl.*
9. *Add dressing, stir gently and serve.*

TIP

To mix it up, try substituting the pine nuts with toasted pecans or raisins.

WHOLE BONELESS
GRILLED CHICKEN

Makes 4 servings

Ingredients:

One 4-pound chicken, completely boneless (ask your butcher)
1 tablespoon olive oil
2 garlic cloves, minced
1 teaspoon fresh thyme leaves
Kosher salt and pepper to taste

Method:

1. *Preheat the GRILL SIDE to 450°F for 10 MINUTES.*
2. *Pat chicken completely dry using paper towels.*
3. *Rub skin on both sides with oil then sprinkle evenly with the garlic, thyme, salt and pepper.*
4. *Place the chicken, skin-side down, on the GRILL.*
5. *Cook for 12 minutes on each side or until internal temperature reaches 165°F on a meat thermometer.*
6. *Remove to a cutting board and let rest for 5 minutes.*
7. *Cut into serving-size pieces, garnish as desired and serve immediately.*

TIP

It is worth going to the trouble of shopping at a grocery store that still has a real butcher on the premises. Make friends with the butcher. They will still go to great lengths to custom-cut meats for you like this chicken.

GRILLED CHICKEN WITH
WHITE BBQ SAUCE

Makes 4 servings

Ingredients:

For the BBQ Sauce:

1 cup mayonnaise

¼ cup apple cider vinegar

¼ cup apple juice

1 teaspoon prepared horseradish

1 teaspoon fresh lemon juice

¼ teaspoon cayenne pepper

Kosher salt and pepper to taste

For the Chicken:

1 (3 pound) chicken, cut into 8 pieces

1 tablespoon canola oil

Kosher salt and pepper to taste

Method:

1. *Preheat the GRILL SIDE to 450°F for 10 MINUTES.*

2. *In a bowl, whisk together all BBQ sauce ingredients; set aside.*

3. *Lightly brush the chicken pieces with oil then season with salt and pepper.*

4. *Place chicken on the GRILL and cook for 7-8 minutes on each side.*

5. *Brush both sides of the chicken with BBQ sauce during the last 4 minutes of cooking.*

6. *Cook until internal temperature reaches 165°F on a meat thermometer.*

7. *Remove, garnish as desired and serve.*

TIP

You might want to make an extra bowl of the white BBQ sauce for dipping at the table. YUM!!!

SPICY WINGS WITH
APPLE GLAZE

Makes 4 servings

Ingredients:

For the Apple Glaze:
¾ cup apple jelly
1 tablespoon apple cider vinegar
⅛ teaspoon cayenne pepper
Kosher salt and pepper to taste

For the Wings:
16 chicken wings, patted dry
2 tablespoons canola oil
Kosher salt and pepper to taste

Method:

1. *Preheat the GRILL SIDE to 350°F for 10 MINUTES.*
2. *In a bowl, combine all apple glaze ingredients; mix well then set aside.*
3. *Lightly brush the wings with oil then season with salt and pepper.*
4. *Place wings on the GRILL and cook for 6-7 minutes on each side or until internal temperature reaches 165°F on a meat thermometer.*
5. *During the last 2 minutes of cooking, brush wings with apple glaze.*
6. *Remove from GRILL then brush with additional apple glaze.*
7. *Serve immediately.*

TIP
Instead of the traditional celery and blue cheese, try serving this dish with apple slices and honey for dipping.

OLD FASHIONED
BBQ CHICKEN

Makes 4 servings

Ingredients:

For the Chicken:
4 pounds meaty chicken pieces such as breasts, thighs and legs
Kosher salt and pepper to taste

For the BBQ Sauce:
¼ cup honey
1 cup favorite bottled BBQ sauce
¼ cup yellow mustard
1 small yellow onion, minced

Method:

1. *Preheat GRILL SIDE to 300°F for 10 MINUTES.*
2. *Thoroughly pat dry the chicken using paper towels.*
3. *Season the chicken with salt and pepper.*
4. *Place chicken on the GRILL and cook for 10 minutes.*
5. *While cooking the chicken, combine all BBQ sauce ingredients in a sauce pan on the GRILL or on the stovetop over medium heat; bring to a gentle simmer and cook for 5 minutes then set aside.*
6. *Flip chicken over and cook the other side for 10 minutes.*
7. *When chicken reaches 130°F on a meat thermometer, brush with BBQ sauce.*
8. *Increase GRILL temperature to 450°F and cook for a few additional minutes until sauce caramelizes and temperature reaches 165°F on a meat thermometer.*
9. *Serve immediately.*

GRILL

BBQ GLAZED
CHICKEN THIGHS

Makes 3-4 servings

GRILL

Ingredients:

1 cup bottled BBQ sauce

⅓ cup honey

1 teaspoon crushed red pepper flakes (optional)

2 tablespoons canola oil

6 bone-in chicken thighs, skin on, patted dry

Kosher salt and pepper to taste

Method:

1. *Preheat GRILL SIDE to 350°F for 10 MINUTES.*
2. *In a bowl, combine the BBQ sauce, honey and red pepper flakes; set aside.*
3. *Lightly brush all sides of the chicken with oil then season with salt and pepper.*
4. *Place the chicken on the GRILL and cook for 7-8 minutes on each side or until internal temperature reaches 135°F on a meat thermometer.*
5. *Brush the chicken with BBQ sauce mixture and continue to cook until internal temperature reaches 165°F on a meat thermometer (continue to apply BBQ sauce and turn the chicken while cooking).*
6. *Remove using tongs and let rest for 3-5 minutes before serving.*

TIP

The reason you don't add BBQ sauce until the internal temperature reaches 135°F is because the BBQ sauce will burn if added too early in the cooking process.

CHICKEN KABOBS
WITH RANCH DIP

Makes 4 servings

Ingredients:

2 tablespoons canola oil

4 garlic cloves, minced

1 tablespoon parsley, finely chopped

3 boneless, skinless chicken breasts, cut into ¾-inch cubes

6 green onions, cut into 2-inch pieces

8 (6-inch long) bamboo skewers

1 cup bottled ranch dressing

Method:

1. *Preheat GRILL SIDE to 350°F for 10 MINUTES.*

2. *In a small bowl, combine the oil, garlic and parsley.*

3. *Thread 3 chicken pieces and 3 green onion pieces in an alternating fashion onto each skewer.*

4. *Brush each kabob with the oil mixture.*

5. *Place skewers on the GRILL and cook for 3-4 minutes on each side or until internal temperature reaches 165°F on a meat thermometer.*

6. *Garnish as desired and serve with ranch sauce for dipping.*

TIP
Try serving these kabobs on a platter with cilantro rice.

CHIPOTLE LIME
CHICKEN BREAST

Makes 4 servings

Ingredients:

4 medium chicken breasts, patted dry

Zest and juice from 1 lime

2 teaspoons dried chipotle chili powder

2 garlic cloves, minced

Kosher salt to taste

1 tablespoon canola oil

Method:

1. *Preheat the GRILL SIDE to 450°F for 10 MINUTES.*
2. *Sprinkle each chicken breast with lime zest, juice, chipotle, garlic and salt.*
3. *Drizzle both sides of the chicken breasts with oil.*
4. *Place chicken on the GRILL and cook for 5 minutes on each side or until internal temperature reaches 165°F on a meat thermometer.*
5. *Garnish as desired and serve.*

TIP

I suggest investing in a good, instant-read thermometer. I like the kind that has a small reference on the back showing what temperatures are correct for meat, poultry, pork, shellfish and fish. You can find these at any kitchen type store.

CHICKEN SLIDERS WITH
APRICOT JAM

Makes 4 servings

GRILL

Ingredients:

1½ pounds boneless, skinless chicken thighs

2 tablespoons canola oil

Kosher salt and pepper to taste

2½ tablespoons Dijon mustard

½ cup store-bought apricot jam

8 soft mini burger buns

Method:

1. *Preheat GRILL SIDE to 350°F for 10 MINUTES.*

2. *Lightly brush the chicken with oil.*

3. *Season chicken with salt and pepper.*

4. *Place chicken on the GRILL and cook for 5-6 minutes on each side or until internal temperature reaches 165°F on a meat thermometer.*

5. *Remove to a cutting board and let rest for 3 minutes.*

6. *Spread 1 teaspoon of each mustard and apricot jam on each bun.*

7. *Chop chicken into small pieces and place 3 ounces of chicken on each bun before serving.*

TIP

You can substitute the chicken thighs with boneless, skinless chicken breast or ground turkey.

BACON WRAPPED SHRIMP

Makes 4 servings

Ingredients:

16 extra large shrimp, peeled, deveined and thawed

Kosher salt and pepper to taste

16 fresh basil leaves

8 bacon slices, cut in half

4 (8-inch long) bamboo skewers

Method:

1. *Preheat GRILL SIDE to 350°F for 10 MINUTES.*
2. *Season shrimp with salt and pepper.*
3. *Wrap a basil leaf tightly around a shrimp.*
4. *Wrap a bacon piece around each basil leaf.*
5. *Slide the shrimp onto a skewer.*
6. *Repeat with remaining ingredients to make 4 shrimp per skewer.*
7. *Place the skewers on the GRILL and cook for 3-5 minutes on each side or until the bacon is a little crispy and the shrimp is opaque.*
8. *Garnish as desired and serve.*

TIP

Don't use extra thick bacon for this dish because the shrimp will be overcooked by the time the bacon is done.

SHRIMP WITH GRILLED
GARLIC TOAST

Makes 4 servings

Ingredients:

For the Shrimp:
1 pound large shrimp, peeled and deveined

2 tablespoons olive oil

2 tablespoons prepared pesto

Kosher salt and pepper to taste

For the Garlic Toast:
2 tablespoons unsalted butter, softened

2 garlic cloves, minced

4 thick French bread slices

Method:

1. *Preheat the GRILL SIDE to 450°F for 10 MINUTES.*
2. *In a bowl combine the shrimp, oil, pesto, salt and pepper; toss to coat evenly.*
3. *Place the shrimp on the GRILL in a single layer, leaving room for the bread.*
4. *Drizzle any extra pesto mixture over the shrimp and cook for 2 minutes on each side or until well browned.*
5. *In a small bowl, combine the butter and garlic; spread evenly on the bread.*
6. *Place the bread slices, butter-side down, on the GRILL and cook for 1 minute on each side.*
7. *Serve immediately.*

TIP
To make a whole easy meal of this recipe, grill some asparagus, sliced yellow squash and onions before starting the shrimp and bread.

GRILLED SHRIMP WITH
POLENTA & PESTO

Makes 4 servings

Ingredients:

⅓ cup prepared pesto

¼ cup canola oil

1 pound large shrimp, peeled and deveined

Kosher salt and pepper to taste

1 package prepared polenta, cut into ¾-inch slices

Method:

1. *Preheat GRILL SIDE to 350°F for 10 MINUTES.*

2. *In a bowl, stir together the pesto and oil.*

3. *Add the shrimp to the bowl and toss to coat.*

4. *Season shrimp with salt and pepper.*

5. *Lightly brush the polenta with oil then season with salt and pepper.*

6. *Place shrimp and polenta on the GRILL and cook for 2-3 minutes on each side or until browned.*

7. *Garnish as desired and serve.*

TIP
I like to grill some cabbage with this shrimp dish.

BBQ

SALMON

Makes 4 servings

Ingredients:

½ cup bottled sesame ginger dressing

½ cup bottled BBQ sauce

4 (7 ounces each) salmon fillets, skin on

2 tablespoons canola oil

Kosher salt and pepper to taste

Method:

1. *Preheat the GRILL SIDE to 450°F for 10 MINUTES.*

2. *In a bowl, combine the dressing and BBQ sauce; set aside.*

3. *Lightly brush the salmon with oil then season with salt and pepper.*

4. *Place the salmon on the GRILL, skin-side down, and cook for 5-6 minutes.*

5. *Turn over the salmon and cook for an additional 5-6 minutes.*

6. *During the last 3 minutes of cooking, baste the salmon with the BBQ sauce mixture.*

7. *Remove salmon to plates, skin-side down, and baste with additional BBQ sauce mixture.*

8. *Garnish as desired and serve.*

TIP
Try a nice mango salad with cilantro with this salmon dish.

SALMON FILLETS WITH
HERBED POTATOES

Makes 4 servings

Ingredients:

4 (6 ounces each) salmon fillets, patted dry

2 large white potatoes, cut into ½-inch thick planks

3 tablespoons canola oil

Kosher salt and pepper to taste

2 tablespoons fresh thyme, chopped

Method:

1. *Preheat the GRILL SIDE to 325°F for 10 MINUTES.*
2. *Lightly brush the salmon and potatoes with oil then season with salt and pepper.*
3. *Place potatoes on the GRILL and cook for 5-6 minutes or until golden brown.*
4. *Turn over the potatoes and place the salmon on the GRILL.*
5. *Cook the salmon for 3-5 minutes on each side or until desired doneness.*
6. *While the salmon is cooking, continue cooking the potatoes until fork tender (sprinkle potatoes with thyme during the last 2 minutes of cooking).*
7. *Remove and serve immediately.*

TIP

I like to serve this dish with a side of tartar sauce.

GRILLED
TUNA STEAK

Makes 4 servings

Ingredients:

2 tablespoons dark sesame oil

1 tablespoon sesame seeds

2 teaspoons soy sauce

1 teaspoon honey

1 garlic clove, minced

1 teaspoon fresh ginger, minced

4 (5 ounces each) tuna steaks, sushi grade

2 bunches green onions, topped and tailed

Method:

1. *Preheat the GRILL SIDE to 450°F for 10 MINUTES.*

2. *In a small bowl, stir together the sesame oil, seeds, soy sauce, honey, garlic and ginger.*

3. *Using a brush, spread mixture over the tuna steaks and green onions.*

4. *Place tuna and green onions on the GRILL and cook for 1-2 minutes on each side or until desired doneness (if you like your tuna rare, it will be done before the green onions).*

5. *Garnish as desired and serve immediately.*

TIP
I like to serve this dish on fluffy rice I make in my rice cooker.

GRILLED WHITE FISH
WITH GINGER

Makes 4 servings

Ingredients:

4 white fish fillets, such as cod or sea bass

2 tablespoons fresh ginger, grated

4 garlic cloves, minced

2 tablespoons soy sauce

2 tablespoons honey

2 teaspoons dark sesame oil

1 bunch scallions, thinly sliced

Nonstick cooking spray

Cooked rice, for serving

Method:

1. *Preheat the GRILL SIDE to 450°F for 10 MINUTES.*

2. *Pat fish thoroughly dry using paper towels.*

3. *In a small bowl, stir together the ginger, garlic, soy sauce, honey, oil and scallion.*

4. *Brush or spoon half of the mixture over all sides of the fish, reserving the rest for serving.*

5. *Apply nonstick spray to the GRILL.*

6. *Place fish on the GRILL and cook for 3-4 minutes on each side or until well browned.*

7. *Remove when fish flakes easily but is still moist inside.*

8. *Serve hot over rice with remaining sauce.*

TIP

Serve this dish with wasabi mashed potatoes. Stir a small amount of prepared wasabi paste into mashed potatoes and enjoy!

SALMON SKEWERS WITH
CUCUMBER SALAD

Makes 4 servings

GRILL

Ingredients:

For the Salmon:
4 (4 ounces each) salmon fillets, cut into 1-inch wide strips
2 lemons, cut into thin slices
8 (8-inch long) bamboo skewers
Canola oil, for brushing
Kosher salt and pepper to taste
2 tablespoons fresh dill, chopped

For the Cucumber Salad:
2 English cucumbers, diced
½ small red onion, diced
3 tablespoons feta cheese, crumbled
2 tablespoons olive oil
2 tablespoons white wine vinegar
Kosher salt and pepper to taste

Method:

1. *Preheat the GRILL SIDE to 350°F for 10 MINUTES.*
2. *Weave 2 salmon strips onto each skewer, alternating with lemon slices.*
3. *Brush skewers with oil then season with salt and pepper.*
4. *Place skewers on the GRILL and cook 3-4 minutes per side (do not overcook the salmon).*
5. *In a large bowl, combine all salad ingredients; toss well.*
6. *Garnish salmon skewers with dill and serve with the cucumber salad.*

TIP
If you think you dislike salmon, try cooking these skewers with your grill placed outdoors. Many people object to the smell of the salmon rather than the taste.

GRILLED
FISH TOSTADAS

Makes 4 servings

Ingredients:

For the Tostadas:

1 pound mild white fish fillets, such as tilapia

2 tablespoons canola oil

1 garlic clove, minced

1 teaspoon ground cumin

1 teaspoon chili powder

Kosher salt and pepper to taste

For Serving:

Corn tortillas, warmed

Salsa

Lettuce

Red onions

Condiments

Method:

1. *Preheat the GRILL SIDE to 450°F for 10 MINUTES.*
2. *Pat fish completely dry using paper towels.*
3. *In a small bowl, stir together the oil, garlic, cumin and chili powder.*
4. *Season with salt and pepper then brush mixture on both sides of the fish.*
5. *Place fish on the GRILL and cook until fish flakes apart but is still very moist (turn once during cooking).*
6. *Transfer fish to a plate and flake apart.*
7. *Serve in warm tortillas with desired toppings.*

TIP
Any mild
white fish will work
well in this recipe.

WOLF'S SAUSAGE
WITH APPLES

Makes 4 servings

Ingredients:

1 Granny Smith apple, sliced

1 Pink Lady apple, sliced

4 sausages or bratwurst, uncooked

Kosher salt and pepper to taste

2 teaspoons fresh lemon juice

1 tablespoon granulated sugar

Spicy brown mustard, for serving

Method:

1. *Preheat the GRILL SIDE to 450°F for 10 MINUTES.*
2. *Sprinkle apples and sausages with salt and pepper.*
3. *Place apples and sausages on the GRILL and cook for 5 minutes on each side.*
4. *Apples are done when brown and sausages are done when internal temperature reaches 180°F on a meat thermometer.*
5. *In a bowl combine the lemon juice and sugar.*
6. *Toss hot apples in the lemon-sugar mixture to coat.*
7. *Serve apples and sausages with spicy mustard.*

PORK LOIN CHOPS
WITH PEACHES

Makes 4 servings

GRILL

Ingredients:

4 pork loin chops, with or without bones

4 fresh peaches, halved

2 tablespoons unsalted butter, melted

Kosher salt and pepper to taste

1 small red onion, thickly julienned

2 tablespoons peach preserves

Method:

1. *Preheat the GRILL SIDE to 450°F for 10 MINUTES.*

2. *Brush the pork chops and peach halves with melted butter.*

3. *Sprinkle pork chops and peaches with salt and pepper.*

4. *Place the pork chops and onions on the GRILL; cook for 4 minutes or until pork chops are browned.*

5. *Flip over the chops, stir the onions and add the peaches, cut-side down, to the GRILL.*

6. *Cook peaches for 2 minutes on each side.*

7. *Cook pork chops on the other side for 4 minutes or until desired doneness and cook the onions until browned.*

8. *Remove all GRILL contents to a plate then brush peach preserves over the pork chops and serve with onions and peaches.*

TIP

If peaches are out of season, apples and apple jelly are just as delicious.

PROSCIUTTO WRAPPED
PORK CUTLETS

Makes 4 servings

Ingredients:

2 tablespoons unsalted butter, melted

4 thin pork cutlets

Kosher salt and pepper to taste

4 fresh sage leaves

4 prosciutto slices

Chopped parsley, for serving

Lemon wedges, for serving

Method:

1. *Preheat the GRILL SIDE to 350°F for 10 MINUTES.*

2. *Brush melted butter on all sides of the pork.*

3. *Season to taste with salt and pepper.*

4. *Place a sage leaf on the center of each cutlet.*

5. *Wrap a slice of prosciutto around each cutlet and secure using a wooden toothpick.*

6. *Place cutlets on the GRILL and cook for 2-3 minutes on each side or until desired doneness.*

7. *Remove and serve topped with parsley and lemon wedges on the side.*

MARTY DOGS

Makes 4 servings

Ingredients:

For the Hotdogs:
4 jumbo hotdogs

4 hotdog buns

2 tablespoons unsalted butter

Topping Choices:
Mustard

Ketchup

Mayonnaise

Hot peppers

Coleslaw

Red onion

Sauerkraut

Pickle relish

Banana peppers

Cheese

Bacon

Method:

1. *Preheat the GRILL SIDE to 350°F for 10 MINUTES.*
2. *Make a cut into each hotdog lengthwise, cutting almost all the way through.*
3. *Butter the insides of the buns.*
4. *Place hotdogs on the GRILL; rotate during cooking until crispy on both sides.*
5. *Place buns on the GRILL, butter-side down and cook until golden brown.*
6. *Remove buns and hotdogs.*
7. *Serve with toppings of your choice.*

TIP
The fun thing about cooking hotdogs is everyone can enjoy their favorite toppings. I like to call this set up the hotdog bar.

SAUSAGE WITH ONIONS  & PEPPERS

Makes 4 servings

Ingredients:

2 large white onions, thinly sliced

½ medium green bell pepper, thinly sliced

½ medium red bell pepper, thinly sliced

½ medium yellow bell pepper, thinly sliced

2 tablespoons canola oil

Kosher salt and pepper to taste

4 sausages or bratwurst, uncooked

¼ cup Parmesan cheese, shredded

1 teaspoon fresh thyme, chopped

Method:

1. *Preheat the GRILL SIDE to 350°F for 10 MINUTES.*
2. *In a bowl, combine onions, peppers and oil; toss well then season with salt and pepper.*
3. *Place the sausages, onions and peppers on the GRILL.*
4. *Cook for 5-7 minutes, stirring onions and peppers frequently.*
5. *Turn sausages over and cook for an additional 5-7 minutes.*
6. *Continue to stir the onions and peppers while cooking.*
7. *Sausages are done when internal temperature reaches 180°F on a meat thermometer.*
8. *Before removing, top onions and peppers with cheese and thyme.*
9. *Place sausages over the onions and peppers on a plate and serve.*

TIP

A nice spicy mustard goes very well with this dish.

LAMB
BURGERS

Makes 4 servings

Ingredients:

For the Yogurt Sauce:
2 garlic cloves, minced

1 teaspoon fresh rosemary leaves, chopped

4 tablespoons Greek-style plain yogurt

For the Burgers:
1 pound ground lamb

Kosher salt and pepper to taste

1 small cucumber, thinly sliced

1 small red onion, thinly sliced

Soft rolls, for serving

Method:

1. *Preheat the GRILL SIDE to 450°F for 10 MINUTES.*
2. *In a small bowl, combine all sauce ingredients; stir then set aside.*
3. *Divide the ground lamb into 4 equal patties.*
4. *Season patties with salt and pepper.*
5. *Place patties on the GRILL and cook for 4-5 minutes on each side or until desired doneness.*
6. *Remove and serve each patty on a roll topped with yogurt sauce, cucumbers and onions.*

TIP
If you find the taste of lamb to be too strong, try mixing it half and half with ground pork.

BISON
BURGERS

Makes 4 servings

Ingredients:

1 pound ground bison or 4 Body by Bison burgers

Kosher salt and pepper to taste

1 large white onion, thinly sliced

4 Cheddar cheese slices

4 soft burger buns

Method:

1. *Preheat the GRILL SIDE to 450°F for 10 MINUTES.*
2. *Divide bison into 4 equal portions then season with salt and pepper.*
3. *On a baking sheet, shape each portion into a 4½-inch diameter patty.*
4. *Place patties and onions on the GRILL and cook for 2-3 minutes on each side; do not overcook, bison should not be cooked to well done temperatures.*
5. *Stir the onions occasionally during the cooking process.*
6. *Place cheese slices on top of each burger during the last 1-2 minutes of cooking.*
7. *Garnish as desired and serve on buns.*

TIP
If using Tony Little's Body by Bison burgers, make sure they are thawed and patted dry.

CHEDDAR CHEESE
STUFFED BURGERS

Makes 4 servings

Ingredients:

1¾ pounds ground beef

2 ounces Cheddar cheese, shredded and divided

Kosher salt and pepper to taste

4 soft burger buns

4 lettuce leaves

4 tomato slices

4 red onion slices

Method:

1. *Divide beef into 8 equal portions.*
2. *On a baking sheet, shape each portion into a 4½-inch diameter patty.*
3. *Using your thumb, make a small indentation into each patty.*
4. *Place ½ ounce of cheese into the indentation of the four patties.*
5. *Season each patty with salt and pepper.*
6. *Top each with another patty and press all around the edges to seal.*
7. *Preheat GRILL SIDE to 350°F for 10 MINUTES.*
8. *Place burgers on the GRILL and cook for 4-5 minutes on each side or until desired doneness.*
9. *Place patties on buns, top with lettuce, tomatoes, onions as well as your favorite condiments before serving.*

TIP
Because I love sweet and salty tastes mixed together, I like to add thin Granny Smith apple slices to the top of my burgers. The taste is great and the crunch is even better.

T-BONE STEAK WITH
HERBED BUTTER

Makes 2-4 servings

Ingredients:

For the Herbed Butter:

1 cup (2 sticks) unsalted butter, at room temperature

1 tablespoon fresh chives, finely chopped

2 teaspoons fresh thyme, finely chopped

1 tablespoon fresh parsley, finely chopped

1 teaspoon kosher salt

For the Steak:

2 (12 ounces each) t-bone steaks

2 tablespoons canola oil

Kosher salt and pepper to taste

Method:

1. *Preheat the GRILL SIDE to 450°F for 10 MINUTES.*
2. *In a bowl, combine all herbed butter ingredients; set aside.*
3. *Brush the steaks with oil then season with salt and pepper.*
4. *Place the steaks on the GRILL and cook for 6-7 minutes on each side or until desired doneness.*
5. *Transfer the steaks to a cutting board and let rest for 3 minutes.*
6. *Slice the steaks into strips if desired, top with herbed butter and serve.*

TIP
Leftover herbed butter will keep in the refrigerator in a sealed container for up to 2 weeks.

CHIPOTLE RUBBED
FLANK STEAK

Makes 4 servings

Ingredients:

1 tablespoon chipotle chili powder

1 tablespoon paprika

Kosher salt and pepper to taste

1 tablespoon canola oil

2 pounds flank steak, trimmed

Method:

1. *Preheat the GRILL SIDE to 450°F for 10 MINUTES.*

2. *In a bowl, combine chipotle chili powder, paprika, salt and pepper; mix well.*

3. *Pat the flank steak dry using paper towels.*

4. *Brush steak with oil then sprinkle chipotle mixture on both sides of the steak.*

5. *Place the steak on the GRILL and cook for 4-5 minutes on each side or until desired doneness.*

6. *Remove to a cutting board and let rest for 3-4 minutes.*

7. *Cut across the grain into thin slices, garnish as desired and serve.*

TIP
Do not cook this meat past medium or it will get tough.

STEAK AND
EDAMAME SALAD

Makes 4 servings

Ingredients:

For the Salad:

3 cups frozen edamame, thawed and shelled

½ cup bottled sesame ginger dressing

1 pint cherry tomatoes, halved

4 green onions, chopped

1½ cups English cucumbers, seeded and chopped

For the Steaks:

2 (6 ounces each) New York strip steaks

2 tablespoons canola oil

Kosher salt and pepper to taste

Method:

1. *In a bowl, combine all salad ingredients; toss to coat.*
2. *Preheat the GRILL SIDE to 450°F for 10 MINUTES.*
3. *Brush the steak with oil then season with salt and pepper.*
4. *Place the steaks on the GRILL and cook for 4-5 minutes on each side or until desired doneness.*
5. *Remove and let rest for 3-5 minutes.*
6. *Divide edamame salad among 4 plates.*
7. *Cut steaks into small pieces and place evenly over the salads before serving.*

GRILLED
POTATO SALAD

Makes 4 servings

Ingredients:

For the Potatoes:

2 pounds small red bliss potatoes, quartered

1 tablespoon olive oil

Kosher salt and pepper to taste

For the Dressing:

2 tablespoons apple cider vinegar

½ cup (or to taste) mayonnaise

2 teaspoons powdered chicken bouillon

1 small yellow onion, diced

¼ cup dill pickle, chopped

1 tablespoon yellow mustard

Method:

1. *Preheat GRILL SIDE to 350°F for 10 MINUTES.*
2. *In a bowl, combine potatoes, oil, salt and pepper; toss well.*
3. *Place potatoes on the GRILL in a single layer.*
4. *Cook for 5-6 minutes or until well browned, flip and cook until just cooked through.*
5. *Transfer potatoes to a large sheet pan to cool.*
6. *In a mixing bowl whisk together all dressing ingredients.*
7. *When potatoes are just warm, fold them into the dressing.*
8. *Adjust seasoning if needed and serve immediately.*

TIP
For additional flavor, try grilling up a few slices of bacon along with the potatoes.

MEXICAN STYLE
CORN ON THE COB

Makes 4 servings

Ingredients:

For the Corn:
4 ears of fresh corn

For Topping:
Mayonnaise to taste

Chipotle powder to taste

Queso fresco cheese, shredded

Parmesan Cheese to taste

Lime wedges

Cilantro, chopped

Method:

1. *Preheat GRILL SIDE to 450°F for 10 MINUTES.*
2. *Place the corn on the GRILL and cook for a total of 20 minutes, turning each corn by ¼ turn every 5 minutes.*
3. *While corn is cooking, place each topping ingredient in separate bowl.*
4. *When corn is done, brush with desired amount of mayonnaise.*
5. *Sprinkle desired amount of chipotle powder and cheese over the corn.*
6. *Squeeze lime juice onto the corn and garnish with cilantro before serving.*

TIP
Try these corn on the cob with the herbed butter in the T-Bone steak recipe on page 54.

MEDITERRANEAN VEGETABLES

Makes 4 servings

Ingredients:

1 small eggplant, sliced ½-inch thick

1 red onion, sliced ½-inch thick

1 zucchini, sliced ½-inch thick

1 yellow squash, sliced ½-inch thick

1 large tomato, sliced ½-inch thick

2 tablespoons olive oil

2 garlic cloves, minced

1 teaspoon fresh thyme leaves

Kosher salt and pepper to taste

Method:

1. *Preheat the GRILL SIDE to 450°F for 10 MINUTES.*

2. *Place vegetables in a mixing bowl.*

3. *Add oil, garlic and thyme to the bowl.*

4. *Season to taste with salt and pepper then toss to coat.*

5. *Place vegetables on the GRILL and cook for 3-5 minutes on each side or until browned.*

6. *Remove and repeat with any remaining vegetables.*

7. *Serve hot.*

TIP

You can use any vegetables you have on hand. This is a great way to use up vegetables from the garden.

RATATOUILLE
KABOBS

Makes 4 servings

Ingredients:

2 green bell peppers, cut into 1½-inch squares

2 red bell peppers, cut into 1½-inch squares

2 yellow bell peppers, cut into 1½-inch squares

2 white onions, cut into 1½-inch squares

2 eggplant, cut into 1½-inch squares

Canola oil, for brushing

Kosher salt and pepper to taste

4 (8-inch long) bamboo skewers

Method:

1. *Preheat the GRILL SIDE to 350°F for 10 MINUTES.*

2. *Alternate the vegetables on the skewers, repeating twice per skewer.*

3. *Brush skewers with oil then season with salt and pepper.*

4. *Place skewers on the GRILL and cook for 4-5 minutes on each side.*

5. *Remove, garnish as desired and serve.*

TIP

This dish makes a wonderful appetizer or can be served over pasta with marinara sauce for a complete dinner.

GRILLED ROSEMARY
FOCACCIA BREAD

Makes 4 servings

Ingredients:

For the Dough:
1¼ cups water
1 tablespoon honey
⅓ cup olive oil
1 teaspoon kosher salt
1 package active dry yeast
2½ cups bread flour

For Brushing:
Olive oil

For Topping:
2 tablespoons fresh rosemary leaves
Kosher salt

Method:

1. *In a stand mixer fitted with the dough hook, combine all dough ingredients.*
2. *Mix for 7 minutes on low speed then turn off.*
3. *Cover the bowl with a towel and let rest for 30 minutes.*
4. *Remove towel and turn mixer back on for 5 minutes (the dough will be very wet).*
5. *Scrape the sticky dough onto an oiled sheet pan.*
6. *Brush the top of the dough with oil.*
7. *Using your fingertips, dimple the dough then stretch it into a rough rectangle.*
8. *Preheat the GRILL SIDE to 300°F for 10 MINUTES.*
9. *Slide the dough onto the GRILL then sprinkle with rosemary and salt.*
10. *Cook for 8 minutes or until well browned.*
11. *Turn over using two sets of tongs and cook for an additional 5 minutes.*
12. *Remove to a cutting board, cut into pieces and serve.*

GRILL

TOMATO & MOZZARELLA
CROSTINI

Makes 4 servings

Ingredients:

1 tablespoon extra-virgin olive oil

1 tablespoon prepared pesto

4 French bread slices, cut on the bias

Kosher salt and pepper to taste

8 small tomato slices

8 fresh mozzarella cheese slices

1 tablespoon bottled balsamic glaze

4 fresh basil leaves, julienned

Method:

1. *Preheat GRILL SIDE to 350°F for 10 MINUTES.*
2. *In a small bowl stir together the oil and pesto.*
3. *Place bread slices on the GRILL and cook for 2 minutes or until browned on one side.*
4. *Remove bread and flip over so that the grilled side is facing up.*
5. *Drizzle each slice with some of the pesto mixture then season with salt and pepper.*
6. *Top each with 2 overlapping tomato slices and 2 cheese slices.*
7. *Place back on the GRILL and cover the GRILL with an inverted rimmed sheet pan (the sheet pan will trap the heat which will melt the cheese).*
8. *After 2 minutes carefully remove the sheet pan using potholders.*
9. *Remove the crostini to a serving plate then drizzle each with the balsamic glaze.*
10. *Top with basil, garnish as desired and serve immediately.*

TIP

For a really cute presentation, cut tiny grape tomatoes into thin slices and arrange them in an overlapping pattern on top of the cheese.

BANANAS FOSTER
FRENCH TOAST

Makes 4 servings

Ingredients:

For the Bananas Foster Sauce:

2 tablespoons unsalted butter, melted

3 tablespoons light brown sugar, packed

2 ripe bananas, sliced into rounds

¼ teaspoon ground cinnamon

2 tablespoons banana liqueur (optional)

For the French Toast:

4 large eggs

1 cup half & half

4 thick slices white bread

Method:

1. *Preheat GRIDDLE SIDE to 350°F for 10 MINUTES.*
2. *While preheating, make the sauce by combining all sauce ingredients, except liqueur, in an omelet pan over medium-high heat.*
3. *Cook sauce until bubbly then remove from heat and add liqueur if desired; set aside.*
4. *In a bowl, combine the eggs and half & half; whisk well.*
5. *Dip the bread slices in the egg mixture to coat then place on the GRIDDLE.*
6. *Cook for 2-3 minutes on each side or until golden brown.*
7. *Remove to serving plates, top with Bananas Foster sauce and serve.*

TIP

To put this over the top, drizzle
2 tablespoons of banana liqueur over
the finished dish.

STRAWBERRY CHEESECAKE FRENCH TOAST

Makes 4 servings

Ingredients:

1 package (8 ounces) cream cheese, softened

¼ cup strawberry jam

1 cup fresh strawberries, sliced

4 large eggs

1½ cups half & half

8 thick French bread slices

3 tablespoons unsalted butter, melted and divided

Method:

1. *Preheat GRIDDLE SIDE to 350°F for 10 MINUTES.*

2. *In a small bowl, combine the cream cheese and jam; stir until smooth.*

3. *Fold the strawberries into the cream cheese mixture then set aside.*

4. *In a shallow bowl, whisk together the eggs and half & half.*

5. *Dip the bread slices in egg mixture and place on the GRIDDLE.*

6. *Drizzle with half of the melted butter and cook for 3 minutes or until golden brown.*

7. *Flip over, drizzle with remaining butter and cook for an additional 3 minutes.*

8. *Remove to serving plates and top with strawberry mixture.*

9. *Garnish as desired and serve hot.*

TIP
This recipe works well with any berries and even diced peaches.

CHOCOLATE FRENCH TOAST SKEWERS

Makes 4 servings

Ingredients:

1 loaf Challah or Italian bread, unsliced

4 large eggs

1 cup half & half

8 (8-inch long) wooden skewers

2 tablespoons unsalted butter, melted

1 cup jarred chocolate fudge sauce, warmed

Powdered sugar

Method:

1. *Preheat GRIDDLE SIDE to 350°F for 10 MINUTES.*

2. *Trim the crusts from the bread loaf then cut in half lengthwise.*

3. *Cut each half into 4 long rectangles to make 8 rectangles.*

4. *In a pie plate, whisk together the eggs and half & half.*

5. *Push a skewer part way into the end of each bread rectangle.*

6. *Dip each skewer into the egg mixture to coat all sides.*

7. *Drizzle butter over the GRIDDLE then place the dipped bread on it.*

8. *Cook for 2 minutes on each side or until golden brown.*

9. *Remove to serving plates then drizzle with fudge sauce.*

10. *Sprinkle with powdered sugar, garnish as desired and serve.*

TIP

If you try to avoid extra calories, you can substitute the half & half with low-fat milk and nonstick spray for the butter.

COCONUT FRENCH TOAST
WITH PINEAPPLE

Makes 4 servings

Ingredients:

1 cup coconut milk

¼ cup granulated sugar

¼ cup low-fat milk

3 large eggs

1 loaf French bread, cut into eight 1-inch thick slices

4 fresh pineapple slices, cut ½-inch thick, peeled

½ cup flaked sweetened coconut

Method:

1. *Preheat GRIDDLE SIDE to 350°F for 10 MINUTES.*

2. *In a bowl, whisk together the coconut milk, sugar, milk and eggs; mix thoroughly.*

3. *Dip the French bread pieces into the milk mixture to coat all sides.*

4. *Place bread on one end of the GRIDDLE.*

5. *Place the pineapple on the other end of the GRIDDLE.*

6. *Cook the French toast and pineapple for 2-3 minutes on each side.*

7. *Remove to plates and top with flaked coconut.*

TIP

Raspberry jam
is a wonderful addition
to this dish.

ABC - 123
PANCAKES

Makes 4 servings

Ingredients:

2 cups all purpose flour

2 teaspoons baking powder

2 tablespoons granulated sugar

1 teaspoon kosher salt

2 cups whole milk

2 large eggs

2 tablespoons canola oil

Food coloring

Plastic squeeze bottles

Method:

1. *Preheat GRIDDLE SIDE to 350°F for 10 MINUTES.*

2. *In a bowl, whisk together the flour, baking powder, sugar and salt.*

3. *In a separate bowl, whisk together the milk, eggs and oil.*

4. *Pour the milk mixture into the flour mixture and whisk until fairly smooth.*

5. *Pour 1 cup of batter back into the emptied milk bowl.*

6. *Stir in the food coloring of your choice until desired color is achieved.*

7. *Pour the colored batter into a plastic squeeze bottle.*

8. *Pour the white batter into a separate plastic squeeze bottle.*

9. *Using the colored batter, pipe letters or numbers directly onto the GRIDDLE.*

10. *Using the white batter, squeeze a pancake over the letters or numbers on the GRIDDLE.*

11. *When bubbles form on the pancake surface, flip over and cook for 1-2 minutes or until golden brown.*

12. *Remove and repeat with remaining batter, making multiple pancakes on the GRIDDLE at the same time.*

TIP

Many of the letters and numbers need to be piped backwards which you will start to notice with practice. You will get the hang of it in no time.

BERRIES & CREAM
PANCAKE ROLL-UPS

Makes 4 servings

Ingredients:

2 cups all purpose flour

2 teaspoons baking powder

1 teaspoon kosher salt

2 tablespoons granulated sugar

2 cups whole milk

2 large eggs

2 tablespoons canola oil

1 package (8 ounces) cream cheese, softened

1 cup powdered sugar

2 cups mixed berries

Method:

1. *Preheat GRIDDLE SIDE to 350°F for 10 MINUTES.*
2. *In a bowl, combine the flour, baking powder, salt and sugar; mix well.*
3. *In a separate bowl, whisk together the milk, eggs and oil.*
4. *Pour milk mixture over the flour mixture and whisk until fairly smooth.*
5. *In a third bowl, whisk together the cream cheese and powdered sugar.*
   (If cream cheese is not pourable, add 1 tablespoon of water and stir until fluid).
6. *Pour ¼ of the batter onto the center of the GRIDDLE and spread into a thin rectangle.*
7. *When batter is mostly dry, spread with ¼ of the cream cheese mixture.*
8. *Press ¼ of the berries into cream cheese mixture on the batter.*
9. *Using a spatula, begin to roll up the pancake, starting from a short end.*
10. *Lift onto a serving plate and repeat with remaining ingredients before serving.*

GRIDDLE

BLUEBERRIES & CREAM
PANCAKE STACKS

Makes 4 servings

Ingredients:

2 cups fresh blueberries, divided

1 package (8 ounces) cream cheese, softened

1 cup powdered sugar

2 cups all purpose flour

2 teaspoons baking powder

1 teaspoon kosher salt

2 tablespoons granulated sugar

2 cups buttermilk or whole milk

2 large eggs

2 tablespoons canola oil

Method:

1. *Preheat GRIDDLE SIDE to 350°F for 10 MINUTES.*
2. *In a bowl, combine 1 cup of blueberries, cream cheese and powdered sugar; set aside.*
3. *In a separate bowl, whisk together the flour, baking powder, salt and sugar.*
4. *In a third bowl, whisk together the milk, eggs and oil.*
5. *Pour milk mixture over the flour mixture and whisk until fairly smooth.*
6. *Ladle 8 pancakes onto the GRIDDLE.*
7. *When bubbles form on the surface, flip pancakes over and cook until golden brown.*
8. *Repeat with remaining batter.*
9. *To serve, layer pancakes with cream cheese mixture and additional blueberries.*
10. *Garnish as desired and serve.*

TIP
You can use inexpensive plastic squeeze bottles to squeeze the pancakes onto the griddle.

ROLLED BREAKFAST OMELET

Makes 4 servings

Ingredients:

8 large eggs

2 tablespoons half & half

Kosher salt and pepper to taste

1 tablespoon unsalted butter, melted

2 green onions, thinly sliced

½ cup cooked and crumbled breakfast sausage

1 cup Cheddar cheese, shredded

Method:

1. *Preheat GRIDDLE SIDE to 350°F for 10 MINUTES.*
2. *In a bowl, combine the eggs, half & half, salt and pepper; whisk until color is uniform.*
3. *Brush butter on the GRIDDLE.*
4. *Pour egg mixture onto the GRIDDLE, avoiding the drip holes.*
5. *Spread out evenly using a silicone spatula; push back if they get close to drip holes.*
6. *Cook until mostly set then scatter remaining ingredients over the omelet.*
7. *Using the spatula, begin to roll up the omelet starting on the short side.*
8. *When you finished rolling up the omelet, lift it off the GRIDDLE using two spatulas.*
9. *Cut omelet into 4 slices, garnish as desired and serve.*

TIP

For an interesting twist, add a bit of marinara sauce, pepperoni and a sprinkle of mozzarella cheese.

EGGS IN A NEST

Makes 4 servings

Ingredients:

1 very large green bell pepper

1 tablespoon unsalted butter, divided

1 small tomato, diced

1 green onion, sliced

4 large eggs

Kosher salt and pepper to taste

Method:

1. *Preheat the GRIDDLE SIDE to 250° F for 10 MINUTES.*
2. *Slice the bell pepper into 4 even and straight rings, ½-inch thick each.*
3. *Place bell pepper rings on the GRIDDLE and drop a small amount of butter into each ring.*
4. *Scatter some diced tomato into each bell pepper ring, reserving some for garnish.*
5. *Scatter greens onions into each bell pepper ring.*
6. *Crack an egg into each bell pepper ring (don't worry if some egg white runs out).*
7. *Season eggs with salt and pepper.*
8. *When most of the egg whites have set, flip over and cook the second sides until desired doneness (for sunny side up eggs, cook until egg white is set and do not flip over).*
9. *Remove, garnish with remaining tomatoes and serve.*

TIP

Since there is extra room on the griddle when making this recipe, add some bacon or breakfast sausages to make a complete breakfast.

BIG BREAKFAST FRY UP

Makes 4 servings

Ingredients:

8 raw bacon slices, cut into 1-inch strips

2 medium Russet potatoes, peeled and diced small

1 small yellow onion, diced

1 cup button mushrooms, sliced

Kosher salt and pepper to taste

8 large eggs

Buttered toast, for serving

Method:

1. *Preheat GRIDDLE SIDE to 325°F for 10 MINUTES.*
2. *Place bacon on the GRIDDLE and toss.*
3. *When some bacon grease appears on the GRIDDLE, add the potatoes, onions and mushrooms.*
4. *Season with salt and pepper and turn frequently.*
5. *When potatoes, onions and mushrooms are browned and potatoes are tender, remove to a platter, leaving the bacon grease on the GRIDDLE.*
6. *Crack the eggs onto the GRIDDLE, one at a time.*
7. *Season with salt and pepper and cook until desired doneness.*
8. *Garnish as desired and serve with toast.*

GRIDDLE

TIP
This dish is a great place to use up leftovers such as cheese, bell peppers, peas, ham or lunch meats.

CARROT LATKES

Makes 4 servings

Ingredients:

2 cups carrots, grated
½ cup yellow onions, grated
¼ cup celery leaves, chopped
3 green onions, thinly sliced
3 large eggs
⅓ cup all purpose flour
Kosher salt and pepper to taste
3 tablespoons canola oil
Sour cream and applesauce, for serving

Method:

1. *Preheat GRIDDLE SIDE to 350°F for 10 MINUTES.*
2. *Pat dry the carrots using paper towels.*
3. *Wrap yellow onions in a double layer of paper towels and squeeze out excess water.*
4. *In a bowl, stir together the carrots, onions, celery and green onions.*
5. *Stir in the eggs, flour, salt and pepper.*
6. *Brush the GRIDDLE with some oil.*
7. *Using 1 tablespoon per latke, drop multiple mounds of carrot mixture onto the GRIDDLE.*
8. *Pat down the tops to slightly flatten and cook for 3-4 minutes on each side or until well browned.*
9. *Remove and repeat with any remaining mixture.*
10. *Serve hot with sour cream and applesauce.*

TIP

It is important to remove any excess moisture from the carrots and onions or the patties will fall apart and not get crispy.

SPAGHETTI PANCAKES

Makes 4 servings

Ingredients:

1 bunch green onions, thinly sliced

2 tablespoons all purpose flour

2 tablespoons Parmesan cheese, grated

4 large eggs

Kosher salt and pepper to taste

¼ cup bell peppers, diced

8 ounces spaghetti noodles, cooked and cooled

3 tablespoons unsalted butter, melted and divided

Method:

1. *Preheat GRIDDLE SIDE to 350°F for 10 MINUTES.*

2. *In a large bowl, combine the green onions, flour, cheese, eggs, salt, pepper and bell peppers; mix thoroughly then add the pasta to the bowl.*

3. *Drizzle some melted butter on the GRIDDLE.*

4. *Spoon mounds of mixture onto the GRIDDLE, pat each down slightly and cook for 4 minutes on each side or until well browned.*

5. *Remove and repeat with remaining mixture.*

6. *Garnish as desired and serve hot.*

TIP

This recipe works well with any leftover pasta and is a great way to use up any leftover vegetables.

CRUNCH-FRIED CHICKEN
DRUMSTICKS

Makes 4 servings

Ingredients:

3 large eggs

¼ cup whole milk

1 cup all purpose flour

2 teaspoons kosher salt

½ teaspoon freshly ground pepper

1 teaspoon dried poultry seasoning

1½ cups panko breadcrumbs

8 chicken drumsticks

3 tablespoons canola oil, divided

Method:

1. *Preheat GRIDDLE SIDE to 325°F for 10 MINUTES.*

2. *In a shallow bowl, whisk together the eggs and milk.*

3. *In a separate shallow bowl, whisk together the flour, salt, pepper and poultry seasoning.*

4. *Place the panko into a third shallow bowl.*

5. *Roll each drumstick thoroughly in flour mixture.*

6. *Dip each floured drumstick in egg mixture then roll in panko.*

7. *Place drumsticks on the GRIDDLE and drizzle with half of the oil.*

8. *Cook for 8 minutes then roll drumsticks by a quarter turn and cook for an additional 8 minutes.*

9. *Drizzle with remaining oil and roll by a quarter turn to cook for an additional 8 minutes.*

10. *Cook on last side for 8 minutes or until internal temperature reaches 165°F on a meat thermometer.*

11. *Remove to a serving platter, garnish as desired and serve hot.*

HAWAIIAN COCONUT CHICKEN BURGERS

Makes 4 servings

Ingredients:

1 pound ground chicken

¼ cup dried pineapple, finely chopped

Kosher salt and pepper to taste

1 cup shredded dry coconut

1 cup panko breadcrumbs

2 tablespoons canola oil, divided

Soft buns

Condiments

Method:

1. *Preheat GRIDDLE SIDE to 350°F for 10 MINUTES.*

2. *In a bowl, combine the chicken, pineapple, salt and pepper; mix well.*

3. *Form mixture into 4 patties that are 4-inches in diameter.*

4. *In a shallow bowl, combine the coconut and panko.*

5. *Press each patty on both sides into the coconut mixture.*

6. *Brush half of the oil on the GRIDDLE.*

7. *Place patties on the GRIDDLE then drizzle remaining oil over the patties.*

8. *Cook for 6 minutes on each side until well browned or until internal temperature reaches 165°F on a meat thermometer.*

9. *Serve on buns with desired toppings and condiments.*

HONEY BBQ TURKEY TENDERLOIN

Makes 2-4 servings

Ingredients:

For the Glaze:
¼ cup ketchup
¼ cup honey
¼ bottled BBQ sauce

For the Turkey:
1 medium turkey tenderloin, patted dry
2 teaspoons canola oil
Kosher salt and pepper to taste

Method:

1. *Preheat GRIDDLE SIDE to 350°F for 10 MINUTES.*
2. *In a bowl, combine all glaze ingredients; stir then set aside.*
3. *Brush the turkey with oil then season with salt and pepper.*
4. *Cook for 3-4 minutes on each side.*
5. *When internal temperature reaches 135°F on a meat thermometer, brush the glaze on the turkey.*
6. *Continue cooking until turkey's internal temperature reaches 165°F.*
7. *Remove and allow to rest for 3-4 minutes.*
8. *Slice and serve.*

TIP
Use the scraper tool to clean the griddle as soon as the turkey is removed. This will make for easier cleanup.

CHICKEN
TOSTADAS

Makes 4 servings

Ingredients:

2 small tomatoes, diced

1 medium white onion, diced

1 small jalapeño pepper, finely diced, seeds removed

4 boneless, skinless chicken thighs, cut into thin strips

1 tablespoon canola oil

Kosher salt and pepper to taste

8 corn tortillas

2 cups queso fresco cheese or Monterey Jack cheese, shredded

½ cup cilantro sprigs

1 whole lime, cut in half

Method:

1. *Preheat GRIDDLE SIDE to 350°F for 10 MINUTES.*
2. *In a bowl, combine the tomatoes, onions and jalapeño peppers; set aside.*
3. *Drizzle chicken strips with oil then season with salt and pepper.*
4. *Place chicken strips on the GRIDDLE and cook for 5-6 minutes, stirring often, or until desired doneness.*
5. *Move chicken to one side of the GRIDDLE then place the tortillas on the other side of the GRIDDLE; warm on each side for about 30 seconds.*
6. *Remove tortillas onto plates.*
7. *Place ½ cup of cheese onto each tortilla then top each with an equal amount of chicken.*
8. *Top with tomato mixture, then garnish with cilantro and lime before serving.*

TIP

Queso Fresco is a soft, white, creamy cheese that originated in Spain and eventually spread to Mexico. I love how the mild saltiness of this cheese pairs with so many dishes.

WOLF'S GRILLED CHEESE SANDWICH

Makes 4 servings

Ingredients:

8 Italian bread slices

4 tablespoons unsalted butter, divided, at room temperature

8 mozzarella cheese slices

8 Swiss cheese slices

Method:

1. *Preheat GRIDDLE SIDE to 350°F for 10 MINUTES.*
2. *Place the bread slices on cutting board.*
3. *Spread ½ tablespoon of butter on each bread slice then flip bread slices over, butter-side down.*
4. *Top each of 4 bread slices with a slice of mozzarella cheese, 2 slices Swiss cheese and another slice of mozzarella cheese.*
5. *Top each with another bread slice, butter-side up.*
6. *Place sandwiches on the GRIDDLE and cook for 3-4 minutes on each side or until golden brown.*
7. *Serve immediately.*

TIP

For an added kick, spread some pesto on the inside of the sandwich before cooking.

GRIDDLED
PASTRAMI ON RYE

Makes 4 servings

Ingredients:

1 pound deli pastrami, thinly sliced

1 cup sauerkraut, well drained

4 ounces Swiss cheese, sliced

2 tablespoons unsalted butter, softened

8 rye or marble rye bread slices

4 tablespoons bottled 1000 Island dressing

Kosher dill pickles

Method:

1. *Preheat GRIDDLE SIDE to 350°F for 10 MINUTES.*
2. *Pile pastrami on the GRIDDLE in an even layer.*
3. *When meat is hot, divide into 4 piles and flip over.*
4. *Top with sauerkraut and cheese.*
5. *Butter all bread slices on one side.*
6. *Turn 4 bread slices butter-side down on a cutting board.*
7. *Divide the dressing between those 4 bread slices.*
8. *Using a spatula, scoop the hot meat stacks onto the dressing-coated bread slices.*
9. *Top each with another bread slice, butter-side up.*
10. *Place on the GRIDDLE and cook 3-4 minutes on each side or until light brown.*
11. *Remove and serve with dill pickles.*

FRENCH DIP SANDWICH

Makes 4 servings

Ingredients:

1 large yellow onion, sliced

4 tablespoons butter, divided

Kosher salt and pepper to taste

1 pound deli rare roast beef

8 Provolone cheese slices

2 baguettes, sliced lengthwise and halved

1 cup good-quality beef broth, warmed

Method:

1. *Preheat GRIDDLE SIDE to 350°F for 10 MINUTES.*
2. *Place the onions on the GRIDDLE and dot with 2 tablespoons of butter.*
3. *Season with salt and pepper and cook until lightly browned, turning often.*
4. *Push onions to one end of the GRIDDLE.*
5. *Butter the bread slices and place them on the GRIDDLE buttered-side down until hot; remove.*
6. *Turn onions over then add the beef to the GRIDDLE.*
7. *Season with salt and pepper then lay the cheese slices over the beef.*
8. *When cheese begins to melt, remove beef and divide between the sandwiches.*
9. *Top with the onions and other bread halves.*
10. *Serve hot with a small dish of beef broth for dipping.*

PHILLY CHEESE STEAK SANDWICHES

Makes 4 servings

Ingredients:

1 bell pepper, julienned

1 large yellow onion, julienned

2 tablespoons olive oil, divided

Kosher salt and pepper to taste

1 pound rib eye meat, shaved thin (ask your butcher)

8 Provolone cheese slices

4 hoagie buns, split

4 tablespoons mayonnaise

Method:

1. *Preheat GRIDDLE SIDE to 450°F for 10 MINUTES.*
2. *Place peppers and onions on the GRIDDLE then drizzle with some oil.*
3. *Season with salt and pepper then cook while turning often for 5 minutes or until lightly browned.*
4. *Remove peppers and onions; set aside.*
5. *Place the beef in an even layer on the GRIDDLE; drizzle with some oil then season to taste with salt and pepper.*
6. *Turn meat frequently using tongs for 5 minutes or until no red remains.*
7. *Use two wooden spoons to break up the meat.*
8. *Place the cheese slices on top of the meat.*
9. *Spread the mayonnaise on the inside of the buns.*
10. *Divide the meat and cheese between the buns and top with the peppers and onions.*
11. *Serve immediately.*

GRIDDLE

GRIDDLED
MINI MEATLOAVES

Makes 4 servings

Ingredients:

1 small yellow onion, diced small

1 large egg

2 white bread slices, torn into small pieces

3 tablespoons whole milk

1 teaspoon kosher salt

½ teaspoon freshly ground pepper

½ teaspoon dried sage

2 tablespoons ketchup + more for tops

1 tablespoon light brown sugar, packed

1 pound ground chuck

8 bacon slices

Method:

1. *In a mixing bowl combine the onions, egg, bread and milk; stir.*

2. *Add the salt, pepper, sage, ketchup, sugar and ground chuck.*

3. *Fold together then divide mixture into 4 equal mounds.*

4. *Cover a sheet pan with plastic wrap then place mounds on it.*

5. *Shape each mound into a 6-inch long rectangle.*

6. *Chill rectangles in the freezer for 30 minutes.*

7. *Remove and wrap each rectangle in 2 bacon slices then secure with toothpicks.*

8. *Press meatloaves into square-sided rectangles to facilitate cooking.*

9. *Preheat GRIDDLE SIDE to 325°F for 10 MINUTES.*

10. *Place meatloaves on the GRIDDLE and cook for 5 minutes.*

11. *Flip over by ¼ turn and cook this side and remaining two sides for 5 minutes each.*

12. *Meatloaves are done when internal temperature reaches 155°F on a meat thermometer.*

13. *Remove and brush with additional ketchup before serving.*

KENTUCKY HOT BROWN SANDWICH

Makes 4 servings

Ingredients:

For the Mornay Sauce:

2 tablespoons unsalted butter

2 tablespoons all purpose flour

Kosher salt and pepper to taste

1 cup whole milk

2 ounces Swiss cheese, shredded

For the Sandwich:

8 bacon slices

4 Italian-style bread slices, thickly sliced

1 pound roasted turkey, sliced

8 tomato slices

Method:

1. *Preheat the GRIDDLE SIDE to 350°F for 10 MINUTES.*
2. *Place a saucepan on the GRIDDLE or on the stovetop over medium heat; add the butter and flour then whisk until all of the flour is incorporated and bubbly.*
3. *Add salt, pepper and milk while whisking constantly.*
4. *When mixture comes to a boil, whisk in the cheese; set aside.*
5. *Place the bacon on the GRIDDLE; cook until browned then set aside.*
6. *Place the bread slices on the GRIDDLE and divide the turkey slices evenly between the bread slices.*
7. *Top each slice with two bacon strips.*
8. *Spoon a generous amount of the Mornay sauce over the bacon.*
9. *Cook for 3-5 minutes or until bread is well browned.*
10. *Remove sandwiches to plates and top each with tomato slices.*
11. *Serve immediately.*

PRESSED CUBAN SANDWICHES

Makes 4 servings

Ingredients:

1 large loaf Cuban bread, split then cut into 4 pieces

¼ cup mayonnaise

¼ cup yellow mustard

24 dill pickle slices

1 pound deli boiled ham, thinly sliced

1 pound deli pork roast, thinly sliced

1 pound deli Swiss cheese, thinly sliced

Method:

1. *Preheat GRIDDLE SIDE to 300°F for 10 MINUTES.*
2. *Place a heavy-bottomed skillet on the GRIDDLE to preheat.*
3. *Spread the mayonnaise and mustard on the bread slices.*
4. *Divide the pickles, pork and ham evenly between the sandwiches.*
5. *Top each with cheese and close the sandwiches with top bread halves.*
6. *Wrap each sandwich in parchment paper.*
7. *Place as many sandwiches as will fit on the GRIDDLE and place the skillet on top to press the sandwiches (press down using an oven mitt so that the skillet sits flat).*
8. *Cook for 5 minutes then remove skillet and flip sandwiches over.*
9. *Replace skillet and cook for an additional 5 minutes.*
10. *Remove and repeat with any remaining sandwiches.*
11. *Cut into long diagonal pieces and serve.*

TIP

Cast iron skillets are the best for pressing these sandwiches. If you have 2 skillets you can do all of the sandwiches in one batch.

WOLF'S FAMOUS MINI BURGERS

Makes 4 servings

Ingredients:

For the Mini Burgers:

12 ounces ground chuck, or higher quality meat

Kosher salt and pepper to taste

4 sharp Cheddar cheese slices, quartered

1 tablespoon unsalted butter, softened

12 silver dollar-size buns

Toppings:

¼ cup iceberg lettuce, finely shredded

4 grape tomatoes, sliced

1 small dill pickle, finely sliced

4 teaspoons bottled 1000 Island dressing

Method:

1. *Preheat GRIDDLE SIDE to 450°F for 10 MINUTES.*
2. *Divide the meat into 12 equal portions then shape into patties.*
3. *Season with salt and pepper then place on the GRILL.*
4. *Cook patties for 2 minutes then flip over.*
5. *Top each patty with cheese then continue cooking until desired doneness.*
6. *Butter the silver dollar buns then remove patties and place on buns.*
7. *Top with desired toppings and serve immediately.*

TIP

If you can't find silver dollar rolls, use bread sticks and cut them into thin rounds.

BLUE CHEESE STUFFED BURGERS

Makes 4 servings

Ingredients:

2 pounds ground chuck

4 ounces blue cheese, crumbled

Kosher salt and pepper to taste

4 soft buns

4 tomato slices

4 red onion slices

4 lettuce leaves

Condiments of your choice

Method:

1. *Preheat GRIDDLE SIDE to 450°F for 10 MINUTES.*
2. *On a plastic wrap-covered surface, divide the meat into 8 portions.*
3. *Shape each portion into a 5-inch patty.*
4. *Divide the blue cheese evenly and place onto 4 of the patties, keeping the edges clean.*
5. *Top each with another patty and press all around the edges to seal.*
6. *Season with salt and pepper.*
7. *Place burgers on the GRIDDLE and cook for 4-5 minutes on each side or until desired doneness.*
8. *Place on buns, add tomatoes, onions, lettuce and condiments of your choice.*
9. *Serve immediately.*

TIP

If you are not a fan of blue cheese, try a mixture of cream cheese and Parmesan cheese in its place.

PIZZA STUFFED BURGERS

Makes 4 servings

Ingredients:

1¾ pounds ground beef

Kosher salt and pepper to taste

16 thin pepperoni slices

4 mozzarella cheese slices

8 fresh basil leaves, chopped

¼ cup bottled marinara sauce, warmed

4 soft burger buns

Method:

1. *Divide the ground beef into 8 equal portions.*

2. *On a baking sheet, shape each portion into a 4½-inch diameter patty.*

3. *Season patties with salt and pepper.*

4. *Top each of 4 patties with 4 pepperoni slices, 1 cheese slice and 2 basil leaves.*

5. *Top each stacked patty with another patty then press the edges to seal (the pepperoni, cheese and basil should be sealed in between 2 patties).*

6. *Preheat GRIDDLE SIDE to 350°F for 10 MINUTES.*

7. *Place patties on the GRIDDLE and cook for 4-5 minutes on each side or until desired doneness.*

8. *Top each with 1 tablespoon marinara sauce.*

9. *Serve on buns and garnish as desired.*

TIP
If you have the equipment to grind your own beef, it makes for a much tastier burger. I suggest New York Strip.

PEPPERONI
PIZZA

Makes two 8-inch pizzas

Ingredients:

For the Crust:

1 pound store-bought pizza dough ball, divided

1 tablespoon olive oil

Toppings:

¼ cup prepared marinara sauce or pesto

1 cup mozzarella cheese, shredded

20 pepperoni slices

2 tablespoons Parmesan cheese, grated

Basil leaves

Method:

1. *Preheat GRIDDLE SIDE to 350°F for 10 MINUTES.*
2. *Stretch each pizza dough ball into a rough 8-inch circle.*
3. *Lightly brush all sides with oil.*
4. *Place a pizza dough crust on the GRIDDLE and cook for 4 minutes or until brown.*
5. *Flip crust over and quickly top with half of the toppings in the order listed above.*
6. *Cover pizza with an upside down skillet or metal bowl to trap the heat.*
7. *Cook for 4 minutes then carefully remove skillet or metal bowl.*
8. *Check the underside of the pizza and remove when it is well browned.*
9. *Repeat with remaining ingredients to make another pizza.*

TIP

If you have 2 small skillets or bowls that will cover the pizzas and fit on your griddle, you can make both pizzas at the same time.

STEAK ROLLATINI

Makes 4 servings

Ingredients:

Nonstick cooking spray

4 cube steaks, tenderized

Kosher salt and pepper to taste

4 cups fresh spinach, divided

1½ cups mozzarella cheese, shredded

¼ cup Parmesan cheese, grated

2 tablespoons olive oil

2 cups prepared marinara sauce, warmed (optional)

Method:

1. *Preheat GRIDDLE SIDE to 350°F for 10 MINUTES.*

2. *Place a strip of plastic wrap on the counter and lightly apply nonstick spray.*

3. *Place steaks a few inches apart on the plastic wrap.*

4. *Cover with another sheet of plastic wrap.*

5. *Pound each steak using a mallet or rolling pin to flatten.*

6. *Remove top sheet of plastic wrap then season steaks with salt and pepper.*

7. *Top each steak with 1 cup of spinach as well as mozzarella and Parmesan cheese.*

8. *Roll up each steak starting at the short end; secure with twine in 3 places.*

9. *Season outside of the meat with additional salt and pepper then drizzle with oil.*

10. *Place steak rolls on the GRIDDLE and cook for 4-5 minutes on each side, turning in quarter turns after every 4-5 minutes or until desired doneness and melted cheese is beginning to come out of the ends.*

11. *Serve hot with marinara sauce.*

GLAZED PORK CHOPS WITH VEGGIES

Makes 4 servings

Ingredients:

4 pork chops, 1-inch thick, patted dry

2 medium yellow squash, cut into ½-inch coins

2 medium zucchini, cut into ½-inch coins

1 tablespoon canola oil

Kosher salt and pepper to taste

½ cup bottled balsamic glaze

Method:

1. *Preheat the GRIDDLE SIDE to 450°F for 10 MINUTES.*

2. *Lightly brush the pork chops and veggies with oil.*

3. *Season with salt and pepper.*

4. *Place the pork chops and veggies on the GRIDDLE.*

5. *Cook for 5-6 minutes on each side or until pork chops are well browned.*

6. *Brush pork chops with balsamic glaze and continue cooking until internal temperature reaches 155°F on a meat thermometer.*

7. *Turn chops over and brush the other side with balsamic glaze.*

8. *Remove chops and veggies from the GRIDDLE.*

9. *Garnish as desired and serve.*

TIP
If you cannot find balsamic glaze, you can make your own by microwaving ¼ cup balsamic vinegar with ⅓ cup granulated sugar until bubbly.

ST. LOUIS STYLE RIBS

Makes 2-4 servings

Ingredients:

1 slab St. Louis cut ribs

Kosher salt and pepper to taste

1 tablespoon soy sauce

1 tablespoon liquid smoke

½ cup favorite BBQ sauce

Method:

1. *Preheat the GRIDDLE SIDE to 250° F for 10 MINUTES.*
2. *Lay a sheet of heavy-duty aluminum foil that is a slightly larger than twice the length of the ribs on the counter.*
3. *Lay ribs, meaty-side up, on the center of the foil.*
4. *Season ribs with salt, pepper, soy sauce and liquid smoke.*
5. *Pull the ends of the foil up and together then crimp tightly to seal.*
6. *Roll and crimp the other open sides tightly to form a sealed packet.*
7. *Place on the GRIDDLE and cook for 30 minutes on each side.*
8. *Increase GRIDDLE temperature to 300°F.*
9. *Carefully open the foil packet and place the ribs directly on the GRIDDLE.*
10. *Brush ribs on both sides with BBQ sauce and cook until sauce begins to caramelize.*
11. *Flip ribs over and cook other side until caramelized.*
12. *Remove and let rest for 5 minutes before cutting into individual ribs and serving.*

CRAB CAKES

Makes 4 servings

Ingredients:

1 pound lump crab meat, very fresh

2 Italian bread slices, crusts removed

2 tablespoons mayonnaise

½ teaspoon fresh lemon zest

2 teaspoons fresh lemon juice

1 teaspoon kosher salt

3 green onions, sliced

1 tablespoon bell peppers, diced small

Method:

1. *Preheat GRIDDLE SIDE to 350°F for 10 MINUTES.*
2. *Pour crab meat into a mixing bowl and remove any shell pieces.*
3. *Place the bread into a food processor and pulse until coarse crumbs are achieved (or tear into very small pieces using your hands).*
4. *Add breadcrumbs to the crab meat in the bowl.*
5. *Add remaining ingredients to the bowl.*
6. *Using a spatula, gently fold the ingredients together.*
7. *Divide the mixture into 4 portions and gently shape into patties.*
8. *Place patties on the GRIDDLE and cook for 4-5 minutes on each side or until golden brown.*
9. *Garnish as desired and serve immediately.*

TIP

The secret to moist crab cakes is the fresh breadcrumbs. They add moisture to the cake. If you use dried breadcrumbs, they pull moisture out of the cake and make it gummy and dry.

SCALLOPS WITH PINEAPPLE SALAD

Makes 4 servings

Ingredients:

4 tablespoons fresh lime juice

6 tablespoons Asian chili sauce, divided

Kosher salt and pepper to taste

16 sea scallops, thawed and patted dry

⅓ cup canola oil

2 tablespoons fresh cilantro, chopped

3 tablespoons white wine vinegar

4 cups fresh baby spinach

1 cup fresh pineapple chunks

¼ cup red onions, chopped

Method:

1. *Preheat GRIDDLE SIDE to 350°F for 10 MINUTES.*
2. *In a bowl, combine the lime juice, 4 tablespoons chili sauce, salt and pepper; stir.*
3. *Brush scallops with sauce then place them on the GRIDDLE.*
4. *Cook scallops for 3 minutes on each side until opaque or until desired doneness.*
5. *In a bowl, combine remaining chili sauce, oil, cilantro and vinegar.*
6. *Add the spinach, pineapple and onions to the bowl; toss to coat.*
7. *Season with salt and pepper then divide the salad between 4 plates.*
8. *Place 4 scallops on each salad and serve.*

TIP

When you buy scallops, remove the small, flat piece of adductor muscle that often lies beside the scallop. Just pull it off with your fingers. It is unpleasantly chewy if you leave it on.

SWORDFISH WITH MANGO SALSA

Makes 4 servings

Ingredients:

1 firm mango, peeled and diced

½ small red onion, chopped small

Juice of 1 lime

Minced jalapeño peppers to taste

Kosher salt and pepper to taste

2 tablespoons fresh cilantro, chopped

2 tablespoons olive oil, divided

4 (6 ounces each) swordfish steaks

Method:

1. *Preheat the GRIDDLE SIDE to 450°F for 10 MINUTES.*

2. *In a bowl, combine the mango, red onions and lime juice; stir well.*

3. *Add the jalapeño, salt, pepper, cilantro and 1 tablespoon oil; set aside.*

4. *Thoroughly pat dry the fish using paper towels then season with salt and pepper.*

5. *Drizzle remaining oil on the GRIDDLE.*

6. *Place fish on the GRIDDLE and cook for 3-4 minutes (depending on thickness of fish).*

7. *Flip over and cook the other side until brown and opaque inside (do not overcook).*

8. *Serve immediately with mango salsa.*

TIP

Before buying fish, check online for the sustainability of that particular fish. My favorite source for this information is the Monterrey Bay Aquarium. They also have a wonderful app if you have a smart phone.

SNAPPER WITH WILTED SPINACH

Makes 4 servings

Ingredients:

4 (6 ounces each) snapper fillets or other white fish

Kosher salt and pepper to taste

2 tablespoons olive oil, divided

1 pound fresh spinach

2 tablespoons chicken stock or water

1 garlic clove, minced

2 teaspoons sesame seeds

Method:

1. *Preheat GRIDDLE SIDE to 450°F for 10 MINUTES.*
2. *Pat fish thoroughly dry using paper towels.*
3. *Season fish with salt and pepper.*
4. *Brush some oil on the GRIDDLE.*
5. *Place fish on the GRIDDLE and cook for 3-4 minutes (depending on thickness of fish).*
6. *Flip over and cook the other side until brown and opaque inside (do not overcook).*
7. *Remove fish and keep warm.*
8. *Drizzle remaining oil on the GRIDDLE then pile on all of the spinach; season with salt and pepper.*
9. *Drizzle spinach with the stock then sprinkle with garlic and sesame seeds.*
10. *Turn the spinach often using tongs (use caution to avoid the steam).*
11. *Cook spinach for 3 minutes or until wilted; remove immediately.*
12. *Divide the spinach between plates, top with fish and serve.*

GRIDDLE

OPENED FACED CATFISH SANDWICH

Makes 4 servings

Ingredients:

For the Sandwich:

4 sourdough bread slices

4 tablespoons unsalted butter

4 (6 ounces each) catfish fillets

2 tablespoons canola oil

For the Garlic Mixture:

1 tablespoon garlic powder

1 tablespoon onion powder

1 teaspoon kosher salt

1 teaspoon freshly ground pepper

For the Coleslaw:

$\frac{1}{3}$ cup mayonnaise

1 tablespoon honey

2 tablespoons fresh lemon juice

2 cups packaged coleslaw mix

Method:

1. *Preheat GRIDDLE SIDE to 450°F for 10 MINUTES.*
2. *Spread 1 tablespoon of butter on each bread slice.*
3. *Place bread slices on the GRIDDLE, butter-side down; cook for 3-4 minutes or until golden brown.*
4. *Remove then set aside.*
5. *In a small bowl, combine all garlic mixture ingredients; stir.*
6. *Sprinkle the garlic mixture on both side of each catfish fillet.*
7. *Brush the GRIDDLE with oil then place the catfish fillets on the GRIDDLE.*
8. *Cook for 4-5 minutes on each side or until desired doneness.*
9. *Place one fillet on each bread slice.*
10. *In a small bowl, combine the mayonnaise, honey and lemon juice.*
11. *Stir in the coleslaw mix.*
12. *Place some coleslaw on top of each fillet before serving.*

SHRIMP
EGG FOO YONG

Makes 4 servings

Ingredients:

6 large eggs

6 garlic cloves, minced

1 tablespoon fresh ginger, minced

1 large yellow onion, julienned

1 bunch green onions, sliced on the bias

3 tablespoons soy sauce

1 tablespoon dark sesame oil

3 tablespoons cornstarch

½ head green cabbage, thinly sliced

8 ounces small shrimp, peeled and deveined

Canola oil, for the griddle

Method:

1. *Preheat GRIDDLE SIDE to 450°F for 10 MINUTES.*
2. *In a bowl, combine all ingredients, except canola, in the order listed above; stir well.*
3. *Lightly brush oil on the GRIDDLE.*
4. *Using a cooking spoon, ladle 6 separate mounds of mixture onto the GRIDDLE and pat each down slightly.*
5. *Cook for 3-4 minutes on each side or until well browned.*
6. *Remove and repeat with remaining mixture.*
7. *Serve hot.*

TIP

This is another great recipe for using leftovers such as peas, green beans or broccoli. If you don't have shrimp, you can use a can of drained tuna.

PANKO CRUSTED
COD FILLETS

Makes 4 servings

Ingredients:

For the Cod Fillets:

4 (6 ounces each) cod fillets

Kosher salt and pepper to taste

2 tablespoons olive oil, divided

Lemon wedges, for serving

For the Panko Mixture:

1 tablespoon fresh parsley, chopped

2 garlic cloves, minced

1 cup panko breadcrumbs

Method:

1. *Preheat GRIDDLE SIDE to 350°F for 10 MINUTES.*
2. *Thoroughly pat dry the cod fillets using paper towels.*
3. *Season to taste with salt and pepper.*
4. *In a shallow dish, combine all panko mixture ingredients; stir.*
5. *Press cod fillets into the panko mixture to cover all sides.*
6. *Brush a small amount of olive oil on the GRIDDLE.*
7. *Place cod fillets on the GRIDDLE.*
8. *Drizzle remaining oil over the cod fillets.*
9. *Cook for 3-5 minutes on each side or until desired doneness.*
10. *Serve with lemon wedges.*

TIP

If you can't find panko, you can use any kind of dry breadcrumbs. However, panko is worth seeking out because it yields the most tender yet crispy crunch.

LAMB T-BONES WITH GARLIC BUTTER

Makes 4 servings

Ingredients:

For the Garlic Butter:

4 tablespoons unsalted butter

4 garlic cloves

Kosher salt and pepper to taste

1 teaspoon fresh lemon zest

1 tablespoon fresh rosemary leaves

For the Lamb:

8 lamb loin chops

Method:

1. *Preheat the GRIDDLE SIDE to 450°F for 10 MINUTES.*
2. *In a food processor, combine the butter, garlic, salt, pepper, zest and rosemary.*
3. *Pulse until the rosemary is chopped into small pieces.*
4. *Thoroughly pat the lamb dry using paper towels.*
5. *Reserve half of the garlic butter mixture for serving.*
6. *Brush the remaining mixture over all sides of the lamb.*
7. *Cook the lamb on the GRIDDLE for 2-5 minutes on each side or until desired doneness.*
8. *Remove to a platter and brush reserved garlic butter over the lamb.*
9. *Serve immediately.*

TIP

Make some extra garlic butter and keep it in the freezer. A thin slice of this butter will really add flavor to chicken breasts. You can also makes great, instant garlic bread.

ROASTED VEGETABLES
IN A FOIL POUCH

Makes 3-4 servings

Ingredients:

4 large carrots, peeled and cut into 1-inch pieces

6 small red potatoes, halved

2 large white onions, peeled and cut into small wedges

6 asparagus spears, peeled and trimmed

2 sprigs fresh thyme

2 tablespoons canola oil

Kosher salt and pepper to taste

Method:

1. *Preheat GRIDDLE SIDE to 300°F for 10 MINUTES.*
2. *Place all ingredients into a large bowl; toss well.*
3. *Place the vegetables on a large piece of aluminum foil.*
4. *Place a same size piece of aluminum foil over the top and seal the edges of the foil all the way around.*
5. *Place the pouch on the GRIDDLE and cook for 7-8 minutes on each side or until potatoes are fork tender.*
6. *Remove the pouch from the GRIDDLE using tongs; let rest for 4 minutes.*
7. *Carefully tear open the pouch and adjust seasoning if needed.*
8. *Serve immediately.*

TIP

Letting the vegetables rest for a few minutes will allow the steam to dissipate. Use caution when opening the foil pouch.

VEGETARIAN ROLLATINI

Makes 4 servings

Ingredients:

2 very large eggplant

3 tablespoons olive oil, divided

Kosher salt and pepper to taste

½ cup sun dried tomatoes, drained

1 cup whole milk ricotta cheese

¼ cup Parmesan cheese, grated

4 garlic cloves, minced

¼ cup pine nuts

½ cup prepared pesto

Method:

1. *Preheat GRIDDLE SIDE to 350°F for 10 MINUTES.*

2. *Top and tail eggplant and cut lengthwise into ½-inch slices.*

3. *Place 8 of the longest eggplant slices on the GRIDDLE.*

4. *Drizzle with half of the oil then season with salt and pepper.*

5. *Cook for 4-5 minutes on each side or until light brown.*

6. *Remove eggplant to a cutting board and divide the sun dried tomatoes over each slice.*

7. *Top each slice with the cheeses, garlic and pine nuts.*

8. *Roll up starting with the short end then secure the ends using twine or skewers.*

9. *Drizzle remaining oil on the GRIDDLE.*

10. *Place rolls on the GRIDDLE and cook for 4-5 minutes on each side, turning in quarter turns after every 4-5 minutes or until desired doneness.*

11. *Remove to plates and serve topped with pesto.*

GRIDDLED
POTATO GALETTE

Makes 4 servings

Ingredients:

4 large Russet potatoes

½ of a small yellow onion

2 tablespoons clarified butter or olive oil

Kosher salt and pepper to taste

Toppings of your choice

Method:

1. *Preheat the GRIDDLE SIDE to 450°F for 10 MINUTES.*

2. *Shred potatoes and onions using a food processor or box grater.*

3. *Place grated potatoes and onions in the center of a clean kitchen towel.*

4. *Gather up the corners and twist from the top to wring out as much moisture as possible (the galettes will never get crispy if moist).*

5. *Drizzle some butter or oil on the GRIDDLE.*

6. *Divide the potato mixture into 4 equal mounds then place on the GRIDDLE.*

7. *Using a spatula, press potatoes down into a thin, even pancake.*

8. *Drizzle tops with remaining butter or oil then season with salt and pepper.*

9. *Cook for 3-5 minutes on each side or until well browned.*

10. *Remove to a cutting board and cut into wedges.*

11. *Serve topped as desired.*

TIP

My favorite toppings are sour cream, apple sauce, smoked salmon or chives.

CREPE CUPS WITH ICE CREAM

Makes 4 servings

Ingredients:

For the Crepes:

1½ cups whole milk

1 cup all purpose flour

3 large eggs

2 tablespoons canola oil + more for brushing

1 tablespoon granulated sugar

½ teaspoon kosher salt

4 muffin tins

For Serving:

Ice cream

½ cup jarred caramel sauce, warmed

Method:

1. *Preheat GRIDDLE SIDE to 350°F for 10 MINUTES.*
2. *In a blender, combine all crepe ingredients, except muffin tins; blend until smooth.*
3. *Brush a small amount of oil on the GRIDDLE.*
4. *Using a ladle, pour about 2 tablespoons of batter onto the GRIDDLE.*
5. *Quickly use the bottom of the ladle to spread the batter thinly using a circular motion to form a 4-inch crepe.*
6. *Cook for 30 seconds then use a small offset spatula to flip crepe over.*
7. *Cook for an additional 10 seconds then remove to a plate.*
8. *Repeat with remaining batter.*
9. *Place 1 cooked crepe into each of 4 oiled muffin tins.*
10. *Preheat oven to 400°F and bake crepes for 10 minutes.*
11. *When done, remove to plates and add a scoop of ice cream to each cup.*
12. *Top with caramel sauce and serve.*

STRAWBERRY SHORTCAKES

Makes 4 servings

Ingredients:

For the Biscuit Dough:
1½ cups all purpose flour
1½ teaspoons baking powder
½ teaspoon kosher salt
1 tablespoon granulated sugar
1½ cups heavy cream

For the Berries:
2 cups fresh strawberries, sliced
3 tablespoons granulated sugar

For Assembly:
Sweetened whipped cream to taste
Powdered sugar, for serving

Method:

1. *Preheat GRIDDLE SIDE to 300°F for 10 MINUTES.*
2. *In a bowl, stir together all biscuit dough ingredients using a fork.*
3. *Stir vigorously until a dough forms that cleans the sides of the bowl.*
4. *Using a small ice cream scoop, divide the dough into 8 mounds.*
5. *Using the palm of your hand, flatten slightly to ⅓-inch thick.*
6. *Place dough on the GRIDDLE and cook for 8 minutes on each side or until golden brown.*
7. *While the biscuits are cooking, stir together the strawberries and sugar in a bowl; let stand to pull some of the juices out of the berries.*
8. *Place 4 of the biscuits onto 4 plates.*
9. *Top each biscuit with some berries and whipped cream then repeat to make a second layer.*
10. *Dust with powdered sugar and serve immediately.*

DESSERT PIZZA

Makes 4 servings

GRIDDLE

Ingredients:

1 pound store-bought pizza dough ball, divided

2 tablespoons unsalted butter, melted

½ cup strawberry jam, warmed until fluid

1 cup semi-sweet chocolate chips

1 cup shredded coconut

1 cup raspberries

1 cup kiwi, diced

1 cup blueberries

Method:

1. *Preheat GRIDDLE SIDE to 350°F for 10 MINUTES.*
2. *Stretch both pizza dough balls into rough 8-inch circles.*
3. *Brush both sides of the dough with melted butter.*
4. *Place both dough circles on the GRIDDLE.*
5. *Cook for 5-6 minutes on each side or until well browned.*
6. *Remove pizza crusts to a cutting board then quickly spread with the jam.*
7. *Scatter the chocolate over the crusts (the heat from the dough will melt the chocolate).*
8. *Top with remaining ingredients, cut into wedges and serve.*

TIP

The refrigerated dough that is packaged in a tube and available in the dairy section of your grocery store is perfect for this pizza.

GRIDDLE

PB&J CHOCOLATE
PANCAKES

Makes 4 servings

Ingredients:

¼ cup cocoa powder

1¾ cups all purpose flour

2 teaspoons baking powder

1 teaspoon kosher salt

3 tablespoons granulated sugar

2 cups whole milk

2 large eggs

2 tablespoons canola oil + more for the griddle

1 teaspoon vanilla extract

Favorite jelly and peanut butter, warmed

Method:

1. *Preheat GRIDDLE SIDE to 350°F for 10 MINUTES.*
2. *In a bowl, combine the cocoa, flour, baking powder, salt and sugar.*
3. *In a separate bowl, combine the milk, eggs, oil and vanilla; whisk well.*
4. *Pour the milk mixture over the cocoa mixture and whisk until fairly smooth.*
5. *Lightly brush a small amount of oil on the GRIDDLE.*
6. *Ladle 6 pancakes across the GRIDDLE and cook until tops bubble.*
7. *Flip pancakes over and cook for an additional minute.*
8. *Remove and repeat with remaining batter.*
9. *Serve pancakes with warm jelly and peanut butter.*

TIP

Any leftover pancake batter will keep in the refrigerator for 2 days. Make sure to stir any leftover batter before using.

INDEX

FOR ALL OF MARIAN GETZ'S COOKBOOKS AS WELL AS
COOKWARE, APPLIANCES, CUTLERY AND KITCHEN ACCESSORIES
BY WOLFGANG PUCK

PLEASE VISIT HSN.COM
(KEYWORD: WOLFGANG PUCK)